The Hare and the Tortoise

Written by Gill Budgell

Illustrated by Beth Hughes

up

ran off

nap

on and on

win

Talk about the story

Ask your child these questions:

1 Who was in the race?

2 Who was winning at the beginning of the race?

3 Why do you think Hare dreamed about carrots?

4 Who won the race in the end? How did he/she win?

5 Do you think that Hare should have won the race?

6 Do you like running? Have you ever won a race?

Can your child retell the story using their own words?